Why Can't I Hear That?

Pitch and Frequency

Louise and Richard Spilsbury

HEINEMANN LIBRARY

Chicago, Illinois

© 2014 Raintree
an imprint of Capstone Global Library, LLC
Chicago, Illinois

To contact Capstone Global Library, please call 800-747-4992,
or visit our web site www.capstonepub.com

Edited by Adam Miller, Sian Smith, and Penny West
Designed by Cynthia Akiyoshi
Original illustrations © Capstone Global Library Ltd 2013
Illustrated by HL Studios
Picture research by Elizabeth Alexander
Originated by Capstone Global Library Ltd
Production by Victoria Fitzgerald
Printed and bound in China by Leo Paper Products Ltd

17 16 15 14 13
10 9 8 7 6 5 4 3 2 1

Library of Congress Cataloging-in-Publication Data
Spilsbury, Louise.
  Why can't I hear that? : (pitch and frequency) / Louise and
Richard Spilsbury.
     pages cm.—(Exploring sound)
  Includes bibliographical references and index.
  ISBN 978-1-4109-6000-9 (hardback)—ISBN 978-1-4109-6005-4
(paperback) 1. Sound—Juvenile literature. 2. Vibration—Juvenile
literature. 3. Sound—Study and teaching—Activity programs—
Juvenile literature. 4. Vibration—Study and teaching—Activity
programs—Juvenile literature. I. Spilsbury, Richard, 1963- II.
Title.

QC225.5.S669 2014
  534'.3—dc23   2013013039

Acknowledgments
We would like to thank the following for permission to reproduce
photographs: Alamy pp. 4 (© David Cantrille), 11 (© Design Pics
Inc.), 19 (© redsnapper); Capstone Publishers (© Karon Dubke)
pp. 7, 7, 9, 12, 13, 16, 17, 17, 20, 21, 21, 28, 29, 29; Corbis p. 23
(© moodboard); Getty Images pp. 10 (Sean Justice/Photonica),
14 (Jeremy Woodhouse/Blend Images), 18 (Travel Pix/Taxi), 26
(Gerard Brown/Dorling Kindersley); Shutterstock pp. 5
(© Menno Schaefer), 15 (© sarra22); SuperStock pp. 6 (Marka),
24 (Tips Images); Design features: Shutterstock © Vass Zoltan,
© agsandrew, © Dennis Tokarzewski, © Mikhail Bakunovich,
© ALMAGAMI, © DVARG,© luckypic.

Cover photograph reproduced with permission of Alamy
(© Grega Rozac).

We would like to thank Ann Fullick for her invaluable help in the
preparation of this book.

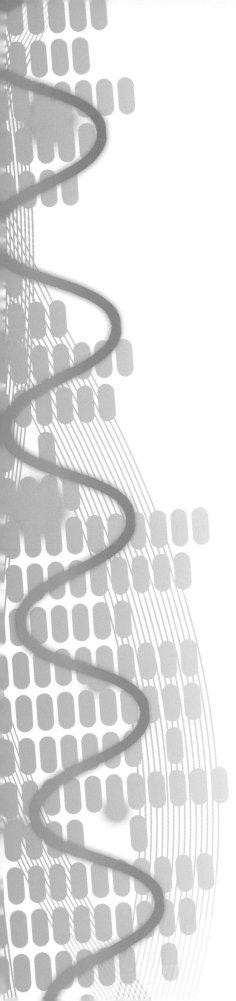

Contents

Some words are shown in **bold**, like this. You can find out what they mean by looking in the glossary.

High and Low

When you sing a song or hum a tune, you change your voice. It goes up and down as you make sounds that are high and sounds that are low. The word for high and low sounds is **pitch**. Listen to some of your favorite music and notice how the sound changes from high to low and back again. Music would be very boring without the highs and lows of pitch!

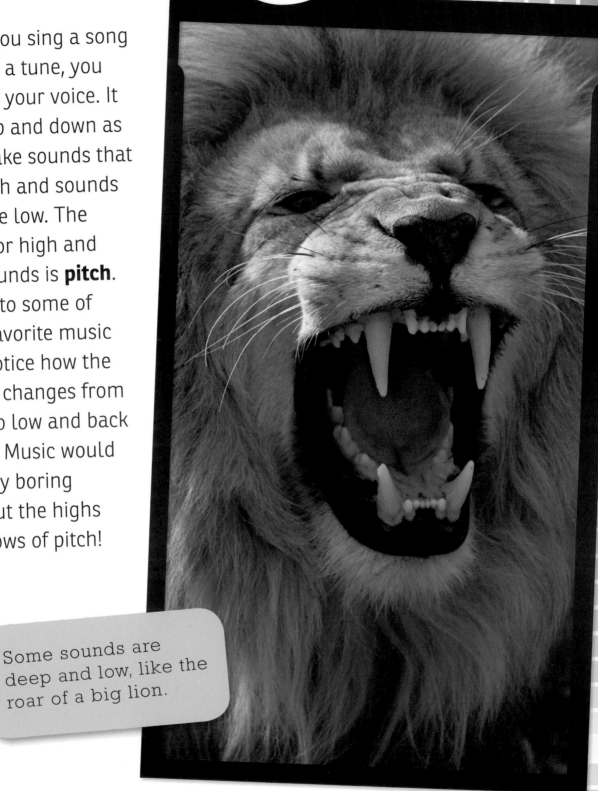

Some sounds are deep and low, like the roar of a big lion.

We hear many different sounds all around us every day. They are all made up of different pitches. A big truck makes a low, rumbling sound when it passes by. A bell on a cat's collar makes a high, tinkling sound. Some people speak in a low, deep voice. Other people have medium- or high-pitched voices.

Listen up!

Listen carefully to the sounds around you. Which are high-pitched sounds and which are low-pitched sounds?

When small birds sing, they make a squeaky, high-pitched sound.

5

Fast and Slow

Things that make sound **vibrate**. They move up and down or back and forth, again and again. When things vibrate, they make the air around them vibrate, too. When these air **vibrations** reach our ears, our ears hear them as sounds.

The **pitch** of a sound depends on how quickly something vibrates. When the string on a guitar vibrates very quickly, it plays a high **note**. When the string on a guitar vibrates slowly, it plays a low note.

The strings on this harp are vibrating to make a sound.

Activity: Testing Vibrations

What do you think will happen when you change how fast a ruler **vibrates**?

What you need

- long plastic ruler
- table

What to do

1. Hold one end of the ruler on the table so that a short end of it hangs over the edge.

2. Hold the ruler tightly and pluck the end hanging over the edge to make it vibrate.

3. Move the ruler so more of it is hanging over the edge. Pluck it again.

4. Repeat step 3. What do you notice?

What happens?

When you pluck a short length of ruler, it vibrates quickly and makes a higher sound. When you pluck a long length of ruler, it vibrates more slowly and makes a lower sound.

Changing Waves

Sound **vibrations** move up and down through the air like waves in the sea. In fact, we call sound vibrations **sound waves**. We count how fast sound waves move by how many times they **vibrate** in a second. The number of vibrations per second is called the **frequency** of the sound.

A high sound vibrates many times a second, so it has a high frequency. A low sound only vibrates a few times every second, so it has a low frequency.

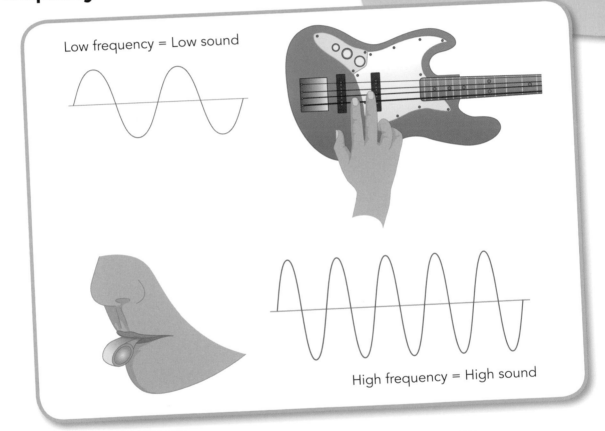

Low frequency = Low sound

High frequency = High sound

Sound vibrations

The slowest vibration human ears can hear is 20 times a second. That is a very low-**pitched** sound. Smoke alarms vibrate 3,000 times a second, making a very high sound!

Activity: Seeing Waves

Can you see how invisible **sound waves** work?

What to do

1 You and your friend should take one end of the spring toy each. Place the two chairs apart so that when you and your friend sit on them, the spring toy is stretched between you.

2 Slide the pole or broom handle right through the middle of the full length of the spring toy to stop it from drooping.

3 Flick your end of the spring toy fast and then slowly toward your friend. Let your friend have a turn, too.

What happens?

You see fast and slow waves of movement through the spring toy. This is like the fast and slow **vibrations** of sound waves.

Playing High and Low

Percussion instruments **vibrate** and make sounds when we tap or hit them. The size of a percussion instrument helps it to make high or low sounds. A big, heavy bell makes a low sound. A small, light bell makes a high sound. Big and heavy things vibrate more slowly because **vibrations** take a long time to move through them. This means they have a slower **frequency** and a lower **pitch**.

A big drum vibrates at a slower frequency than a small drum. That is why it makes a lower sound.

Which end of this xylophone do you think plays the higher notes?

Some percussion instruments are made of parts with different pitches. Glockenspiels and xylophones have long bars and short bars. Long bars vibrate more slowly than short bars. So, the shorter bars on an instrument play the higher **notes**, and the longer bars play the lower notes.

Low, not soft!

Just because something vibrates more slowly, it does not mean it is quieter. You can use a bass drum or a big bell to play low notes very loudly.

Activity: Make a Xylophone

Do you think that a bottle with less water or more water will have the higher **pitch**?

What to do

1 Fill each bottle with a different amount of liquid.

What you need
- seven empty clear glass bottles (the exact same size and shape)
- water
- food coloring
- wooden stick or pencil

2 Add food coloring to the bottles to make the different water levels easier to see.

2

3 Line the bottles up on a table in a row. Make sure none of the bottles is touching. Tap the bottles above the water line with the stick. Which bottle makes the highest sound? Which makes the lowest sound? Why do you think that is?

Try this!

Now try to use your glass xylophone to play a tune!

What happens?

When you hit an empty bottle, it **vibrates** and makes a sound. When you add water to a bottle, the water slows down the **vibrations** in the glass. The bottle with the least amount of water vibrates the fastest. It has the highest pitch. The bottle with the most water vibrates the slowest. It has the lowest pitch.

Playing with Strings

String instruments make sounds when their strings **vibrate**. Different string instruments make high and low **notes** in different ways. A harp has some short and some long strings. They play different notes. Long strings vibrate more slowly and make lower-**pitched** sounds than short strings.

Strings on a violin or a guitar are all the same length, but some strings are heavier and thicker than the others. The heavier, thicker strings vibrate more slowly and make lower notes. The thinner, lighter strings vibrate more quickly and make higher notes.

The biggest string instruments in this band have longer, thicker, heavier strings than the rest. That is why they make the deepest sounds.

Tall and short

The lowest string on a tall double bass vibrates 40 times per second. The highest string on a violin vibrates 440,000 times per second!

We can change a string's pitch by making it shorter. When we hold a string firmly down on its **fingerboard**, this shortens the length of the string that can vibrate. Shorter strings vibrate at a faster **frequency** and make a higher-pitched sound. Try it on a real guitar!

Players can make a string play a higher note by pressing their fingers down to shorten the string.

Activity: Testing Strings

Make a string instrument to test how thickness and length affect **frequency**.

What to do

1 Begin with the widest rubber band and stretch it around the sheet. Then choose the next-widest rubber band and place it just under 1 inch (2 centimeters) away from the first rubber band, stretched around the sheet.

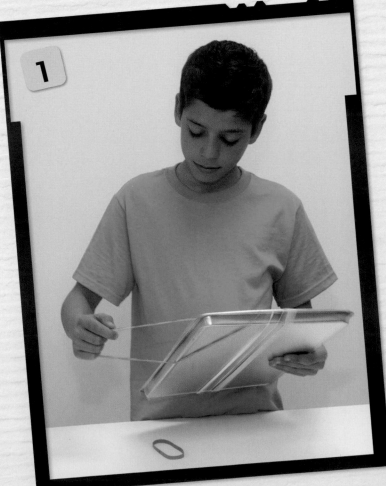

2 Continue until all the rubber bands are on the sheet. These are your instrument's strings.

3 If you pluck each string in turn, which do you think will make the highest and which will make the lowest **note**? Pluck each string. Were you right?

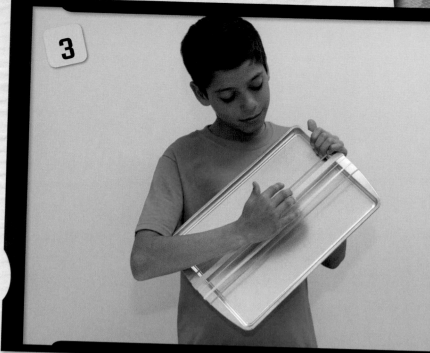

3

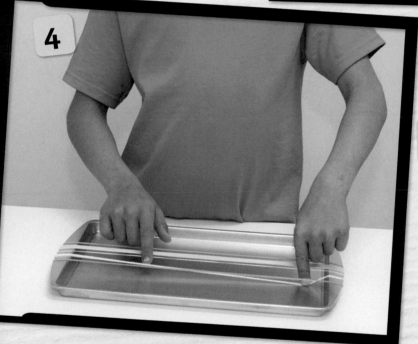

4

4 Now pluck one of your strings and then press down on it firmly, so that it touches the bottom of the baking sheet. Pluck it again. What happens?

What happens?

The heavy, thick strings make lower notes than the lighter, thinner strings, just like on a real string instrument. When you press down on the rubber band at one end, you make the part of the string that **vibrates** shorter. The shorter length vibrates faster, so it makes a higher-**pitched** sound than it did before.

Tuning Tubes

Recorders, trumpets, and other wind instruments have **hollow** tubes that you blow into. They make sound when air inside the tube **vibrates**. Longer tubes have a longer length of air that vibrates more slowly. They make a lower-**pitched** sound. Shorter tubes have a shorter length of air that vibrates more quickly. They make a higher-pitched sound.

Pan pipes

Pan pipes are wind instruments made from hollow plant stems (the part that holds up the leaves and flowers) of different lengths. When you blow across the top of these tubes, each one plays a different note. Pan pipes have been played for thousands of years in the Andes Mountains of South America.

We mostly change the pitch on a wind instrument by making the tubes of air longer and shorter. To do this, we cover and uncover holes on the side of the tube. This changes the length that the air must travel when vibrating and makes the **notes** lower and higher. On a recorder, we make notes lower by putting fingers over holes along the top of the instrument. This means the air has to travel farther before some of it can escape through a hole.

You press buttons called keys to change notes on a tuba. These cover and uncover holes, to change how much air flows through the different tubes.

Activity: Pan Pipes

Make your own pan pipes.

What you need
- eight straight straws
- ruler
- scissors
- masking tape
- cardboard
- pen

What to do

1 Use the ruler and pen to mark a different length on each of the eight straws:

8 inches (19.5 centimeters),
6.5 inches (17 centimeters),
6 inches (15.5 centimeters),
5.5 inches (14.5 centimeters),
5 inches (13 centimeters),
4.5 inches (11.5 centimeters),
4 inches (10 centimeters),
and 3.5 inches (9.5 centimeters).

2 Cut the eight straws to these lengths.

1

3 Measure and cut out a piece of cardboard about 5 inches (12 centimeters) long and 1 inch (3 centimeters) wide.

4 Line up the straws along the cardboard, about half an inch (1 centimeter) apart. Arrange the straws in order, from the longest to the shortest. Keep the tops of the straws in a straight line. Tape the straws to the cardboard.

4

5 Write the numbers 1 to 8 on the straws, with 1 being the longest.

6

6 Blow air across the straws, one at a time. Keep trying until you make a good sound.

Try this!

Blow these numbers in turn to play "Twinkle, Twinkle, Little Star."

```
1 1 5 5 6 6 5
4 4 3 3 2 2 1
5 5 4 4 3 3 2
5 5 4 4 3 3 2
1 1 5 5 6 6 5
4 4 3 3 2 2 1
```

Make up some songs. Use the numbers to help you write your songs.

What happens?

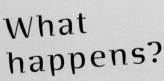

You should hear that the longer the straw, the lower the **pitch**, and the shorter the straw, the higher the pitch.

Changing Voices

Our voices work a bit like a wind instrument. When you want to make a sound, you push air from your **lungs** up through a tube in your throat called the **trachea**. At the top of the trachea is your voice box, or **larynx**. The air pushes soft folds of skin called **vocal cords** in the larynx so they **vibrate** and make sounds. To make a higher sound, we tighten the vocal cords and make them smaller. Then they vibrate faster and make a higher sound. To make lower sounds, we loosen the cords, so they are longer. Longer vocal cords take more time to vibrate back and forth, so they make a lower sound.

We change the shape of our vocal cords to change the frequency at which they vibrate. This changes the pitch of our voice.

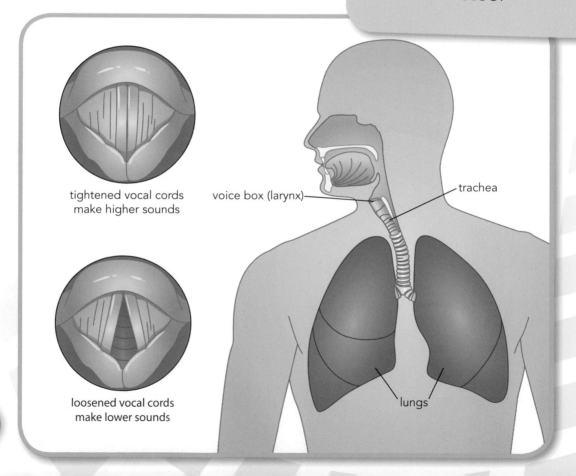

tightened vocal cords make higher sounds

loosened vocal cords make lower sounds

voice box (larynx)

trachea

lungs

To help you see how this works, blow up a balloon. Pull the open end tight and let the air rush out to make a high noise. Then loosen the mouth of the balloon to make a lower-**pitched** sound. This is a bit like the way your vocal cords work.

We do not have to think about making our vocal cords shorter and longer. It just happens when we talk or sing.

23

Animal Frequencies

Many animals make sounds using **vocal cords**. Some use different **pitches** and **frequencies** to say different things. When a lion makes a deep growl to warn off other animals, its vocal folds **vibrate** about 20 times a second. When a dachshund dog makes a high, whining sound to say hello, its vocal folds vibrate 1,000 times a second!

Prairie dog pitches

When prairie dogs see a dangerous animal, they shout an alarm call to tell others to run. The amazing thing is they use different frequencies and pitches to describe different animals. They use many different words, including *human*, *hawk*, and *coyote*, and scientists think they even have words to describe things like size and color!

Bats use sounds to help them hunt and find their way in the dark. They make very high-frequency squeaks by tightening their **larynx**. The squeaks spread out into a cone of sound like light from a flashlight. When the sound hits an object like a moth, an **echo** bounces back to the bat's big ears. The bat can tell where the moth is by figuring out where the echoes come from and how long it takes them to return. This is called **echolocation**.

One reason bats use high-frequency sounds is that these stand out from other noises heard at night, which are mostly at low frequency.

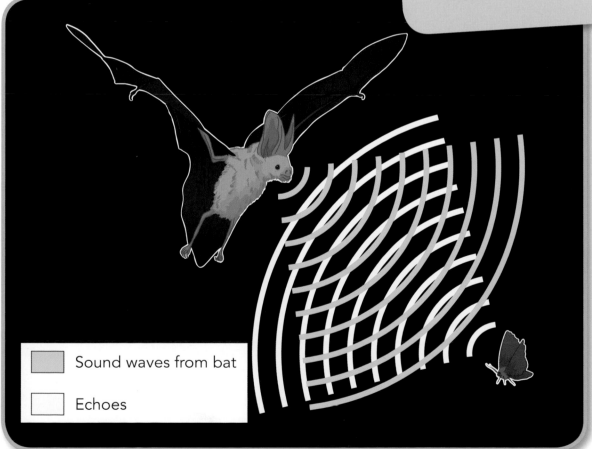

Sound waves from bat

Echoes

Ultrasound

Bats can hear higher sounds than any other land animal. Humans cannot hear sounds over 20,000 **vibrations** per second. High-**frequency** sounds like this are called **ultrasound**. Elephants make very low-frequency rumbling sounds that are too low for us to hear. As we get older, our ability to hear low sounds weakens a little, and our ability to hear high sounds weakens a lot.

Dogs can hear higher-frequency sounds than we can. That is why they can hear dog whistles and we cannot!

We cannot hear ultrasound, but we use it in different ways. People on ships and submarines use ultrasound to find fish, shipwrecks, or the seabed. A ship sends out a high-frequency ultrasound. This bounces off the group of fish back to a machine that detects the **echo**. The machine uses the time taken for the echo to travel back to figure out how deep in the water the fish are.

Fishing boats use the echoes from high-frequency vibrations to help them find fish.

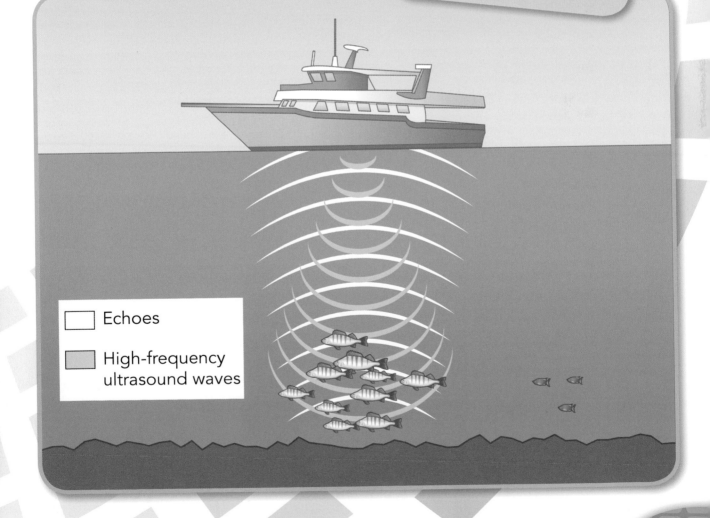

Echoes

High-frequency ultrasound waves

Activity: Hearing Echoes

Explore the way that sounds can bounce back or **echo**.

What to do

1 Tape down the tubes on a table so they are angled toward the edge of the table and toward each other in a V shape, but not touching. Ideally, the table should be in a quiet place outside or with plenty of space around it, away from other objects.

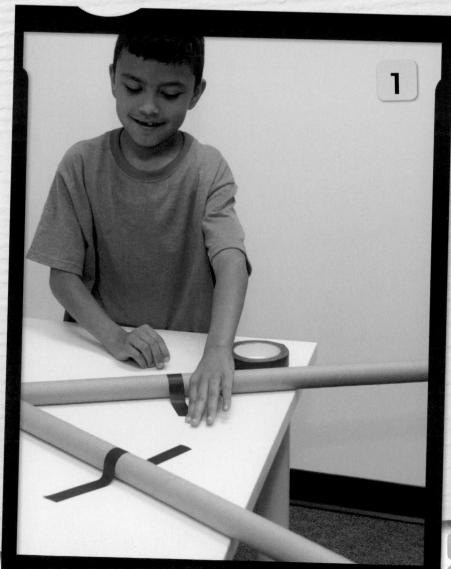

1

2 Put the watch just inside the end of one tube. Cover one ear and put the other ear to the end of the other tube. What can you hear?

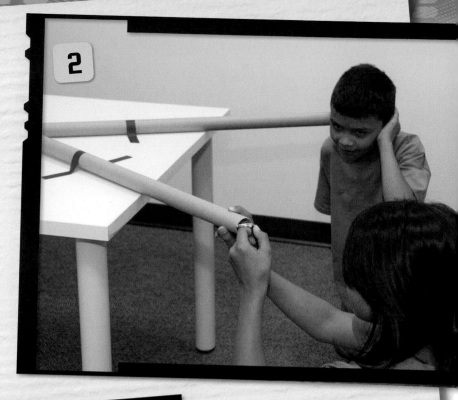

3 Tape the metal tray to the table so that most of the surface faces the ends of the tubes about 12 inches (30 centimeters) away.

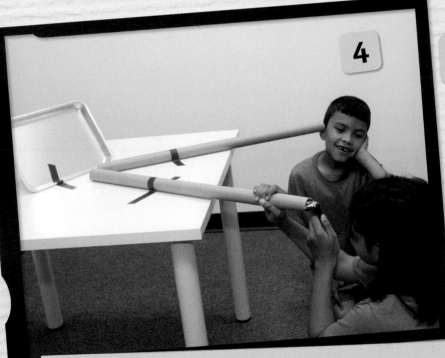

4 Put your ear to the end of the tube without the watch and listen again. What can you hear?

What happens?

When you listen the first time, you probably will not hear the ticking of the watch. But the second time, sound should bounce off the metal tray and come up the other tube. You made an echo! If it did not work, try changing the angle your tube makes with the tray.

Glossary

echo sound that is repeated as the sound waves reflect off a surface

echolocation process of using sound to find things

fingerboard strip of wood on the neck of a stringed instrument against which the strings are pressed to make different notes

frequency number of vibrations in a sound; the number of times a sound wave vibrates in a second

hollow something that has a hole or empty space inside it

larynx area at the top of the throat that contains the vocal cords

lung body part found in the chest that is used for breathing

note single sound of a particular pitch

percussion type of musical instrument that you play by hitting it

pitch how low (deep) or high (squeaky) a sound is

sound wave vibration in the air that we hear as sound

trachea tube in the neck and chest that carries air to and from the lungs

ultrasound sound that is higher than humans can hear

vibrate, **vibration** move back and forth or up and down very quickly, again and again

vocal cords body parts that are stretched across the larynx in the throat. They vibrate when air goes past them to make the sound of our voice.

Find Out More

Books

Mahaney, Ian F. *Sound Waves* (Energy in Action). New York: PowerKids, 2007.

McGregor, Harriet. *Sound* (Sherlock Bones Looks at Physical Science). New York: Windmill, 2011.

Sohn, Emily. *Adventures in Sound with Max Axiom*, *Super Scientist* (Graphic Science). Mankato, Minn.: Capstone, 2007.

Spilsbury, Richard, and Louise Spilsbury. *What Is Sound?: Exploring Sound with Hands-on Activities* (Science Adventures). Berkeley Heights, N.J.: Enslow, 2008.

Internet sites

Use Facthound to find Internet sites related to this book. All of the sites on Facthound have been researched by our staff.

Here's all you do:

Visit www.facthound.com

Type in this code: 9781410960009

Index